This Document Contains the

FINAL WISHES

of:

_____

Last Updated on

_____

Date

Final Wishes
2nd Edition

Thank you for choosing to leave a legacy of peace and order by documenting your final wishes and, most importantly, making those wishes known to the ones you trust to carry them out.

Because death is an important—and certain—event in all our lives, this workbook is designed to help your loved ones determine how to proceed upon your death. In the event you have minor children, adult dependents, or pets that need immediate attention upon your death, this edition provides space for indicating whom should be contacted in those instances.

Also, an entirely new section appears in this edition: Important Papers, Information, and Artifacts. This section allows you to document your digital information—that is, user IDs and passwords for accessing electronic devices, email services, social media, entertainment sites, online banking, and cloud-based documents and photographs.

Kudos to you for taking the first step toward leaving a legacy of peace and order by purchasing this workbook. However, this workbook will not write itself! This is not easy work, but the legacy you leave behind will make it all worth it.

Lisa Caraway Oliver, EdD, GC-C
Life Transitions Educator | Certified Grief Counselor
Principal, Dr. Lisa Oliver, LLC

Table of Contents

Copies of This Document Have Been Given To:

1. _____

_____
(Provide complete name, address, phone number and email address)

2. _____

_____
(Provide complete name, address, phone number and email address)

3. _____

_____
(Provide complete name, address, phone number and email address)

4. _____

_____
(Provide complete name, address, phone number and email address)

5. _____

_____
(Provide complete name, address, phone number and email address)

Part I:
What Needs to Happen Once Your Death Has Been Pronounced

Information About Me*†

Full Name
_____

Maiden Name
_____

Date of Birth   Birthplace
_____

Sex   Race
_____

Full Name of Father   Birthplace of Father
_____

Full Maiden Name of Mother   Birthplace of Mother
_____

Social Security Number
_____

Marital Status   Spouse's Name
_____

Occupation   Employer
_____

Type of Business   Years at Occupation   Education
_____

Residence Address
_____

City, State, Zip
_____

Country   Years in Country
_____

Military Service (year)   to (year)   Branch of Service
_____

Served Where?

The information requested here should serve as a guideline. The information required for a Death Certificate varies from state to state.

†*Veterans: Benefits may be available to cover some or all expenses upon your death. See page 51 for details.*

Which Mortuary Service to Contact

When you die, a loved one must first determine which mortuary to call. You can relieve stress on loved ones by making this decision on your own in advance.

_____
Mortuary

_____
Contact Person

_____
Address

_____
City, State, Zip

_____
Telephone

_____
Fax

_____
Website

Have funeral arrangements been pre-paid?　☐ **Yes**　☐ **No**

_____
Where is the pre-paid plan contract located?

Notes:

_____

_____

_____

_____

_____

_____

_____

_____

Care of Your Dependents

If you are responsible for minor children or dependent adults, your will should specify the name of the guardian who will care for them upon your death. The probate of a will takes a few weeks to a few years, depending on the size of the estate and whether the will is contested. Suffice it to say that when your death occurs, the care of minor children and/or dependent adults must be addressed immediately.

First Contact Person

_____
Name

_____
Address

_____
City, State, Zip

_____
Telephone

_____
Email Address

Second Contact Person

_____
Name

_____
Address

_____
City, State, Zip

_____
Telephone

_____
Email Address

Care of Your Pets

According to Everplans.com, only 9% of people with wills include provisions for their cats, dogs, or exotic birds.* Once you have chosen someone to care for your pet, be sure to ask them if they are willing to do so if something happens to you. It takes more than a will to decide what happens to a beloved pet; **you must have the cooperation** of the people involved.

_____
Pet Care Provider

_____
Contact Person

_____
Address

_____
City, State, Zip

_____
Phone Number

_____
Email Address

If you are unable appoint a caregiver, Everplans.com lists several lifetime care centers that can care for your pet. This list is by no means exhaustive; consider searching for local options.

2nd Chance 4 Pets

If you are just starting this process and weighing your options, contact the volunteers at 2nd Chance 4 Pets. While this nonprofit does not provide homes for pets, it specializes in saving the pets of deceased owners from kill shelters. The volunteers can answer any questions you have about lifetime care facilities and help point you to one that makes sense for your pet. They have ties to homes all over the U.S., connections that may prove useful.

Circle Star Pet Resort

This Texas sanctuary promises space for dogs, horses, donkeys, llamas, and cows. Once you reserve a spot, you pay according to a fixed plan but can cancel any time. The property includes a large ranch-style home with a patio, large grassy areas, and a pool. Onsite "den moms" play with and supervise your pet 24/7. Plus, all the basics (food, veterinary care, etc.) are included. Also, keep an eye on the Circle Star website—facilities for cats, pigs, and birds are currently underway.

_____

* In the United States, 68% of people do not have a will (Weisbord & Horton, 2021)

Animal Friends

Animal Friends is a no-kill shelter in Pittsburgh, PA, with a special "society" open to cats and dogs. Donors who give $5,000 or more to the group are eligible to enroll in the Lifesavers Society, a program that pledges to care for your pet after you pass. Upon your passing, Animal Friends will immediately take in your dog or cat and then care for them personally until the shelter finds a new home that abides by its adoption guidelines. To get the ball rolling, you will need to fill out a declaration of intent, available on the Animal Friends website.

Dancing Creek Farm

Located in Virginia near the North Carolina state line, this sprawling farm specializes in long-term dog boarding. Dancing Creek emphasizes that it is no run-of-the-mill kennel. The owners live on the property and have handlers watching the dogs 7 days a week. Your dog will stay in an air-conditioned cabin, have daily access to large outdoor play areas, and enjoy pampering thanks to the weekly warm lavender towel wipe-down and massage. The lifetime care program requires a Trust, but the owners can talk you through your options. Learn more here.

Peace of Mind Dog Rescue

This California nonprofit requires a Pet Trust before you can enroll in its perpetual care program. Once that is set up, Peace of Mind makes a lifelong commitment to your dog. They will put up your dog in a boarding house with regular walks while they search for a suitable foster or permanent home. The new family will be determined by the "pet profile" you set up, which lists your dog's likes, dislikes, health history, habits, and vet records. Peace of Mind does not discriminate against old or sick dogs, but it does have to determine that your pet qualifies before they can commit. If this sounds like your best option, you should reach out ASAP—and give your lawyer a call while you are at it. The Trust will require some legal expertise.

Pet Pride of New York

Pet Pride of New York is a cats-only sanctuary. The shelter is located on 15 acres of wooded property in Victor, NY. Any cat staying there receives their own large cage with a litter box, water, toys, food, and a bed. They also get let out each day to play—and if they have pals on the premises, they will be let out together. To reserve a space for your feline, you will need to sign a contract pledging to set aside a certain dollar amount in your will for the nonprofit. You can peruse the fine print in this online copy.

Pet Peace of Mind

This national nonprofit works with hospices, home health agencies, and hospitals to keep "patients and their pets together at a time when they need each other the most." They assist with pet care while patients are alive and provide help with re-homing to ensure pets find new forever homes. Check out the video on their site explaining the inspiration behind Pet Peace of Mind.

Disposition of My Body

There are many options to consider when making decisions about the final disposition of your body. A few of these options are described below.

Burial

Burial is the traditional choice. It can be done directly, with no viewing or ceremonies, or with any combination of viewing, ceremony, and graveside service. It usually requires you to pay for: a casket; cemetery plot; fees to open and close the grave; cemetery endowment (upkeep); and a marker, monument, or headstone. Though most burials are below ground, another (and usually more expensive) option is above-ground burial in a mausoleum.

Direct burial is the least expensive option: The mortuary files the necessary paperwork, places the unembalmed body in a casket, and takes the remains to a cemetery for burial, usually within one day. This is often accompanied by a simple graveside service. This alternative eliminates expenses for embalming and some expenses for mortuary facilities, and most families who opt for direct burial choose a lower-priced casket.

Embalming is the art and science of preserving human remains by treating them with chemicals to forestall decomposition. The intention is to keep the remains suitable for public display at a funeral, for religious reasons, or for medical and/or scientific purposes such as their use as anatomical specimens.

Cremation

Cremation is a popular choice. Usually, neither a casket nor embalming is required, but if the body must be held for several days, refrigeration or embalming may be necessary. Cremation, like burial, can be direct or can occur after a funeral. It is also possible to have an embalming, viewing, and ceremony followed by cremation. Some mortuaries offer rental caskets for a viewing ceremony prior to cremation, while others sell modest caskets designed for cremation. Cremation also allows flexibility as to when or where services are held; many families now hold memorial services in their own homes or at the deceased's favorite place.

Cremated remains ("cremains") may be scattered, kept at home, buried in a cemetery, or interred in a columbarium (an above-ground structure containing permanent niches). Burial of cremated remains in a cemetery or placement in a columbarium adds to the overall cost of final arrangements.

Aquamation (or Resomation)

Aquamation, or Resomation, is heralded as the new, truly environmentally friendly alternative to cremation or burial. According to U.S. Funerals Online, "using a natural process called alkaline hydrolysis, Aquamation uses just 10% of the energy used during a cremation process and there are NO air emissions. No organic matter can be discharged from cremation chimneys, and no methane gas or toxic chemicals can leak from a burial casket and can seep into the water table" (Marsden-Ille, 2021).

Disposition of My Body (continued)

Donation

Whether a body is to be buried or cremated, part or all the remains can first be donated to improvethe quality of life of others or to offer the gift of life itself. Donation of at least some body parts is an option for almost anyone, regardless of age or medical history. Whether donation is right for you is a matter of personal choice.

Individuals can donate organs, tissues, or their whole bodies. If you wish to become a donor, let your loved ones know, enroll with the local organ-donor registry, and have your donor status noted on your driver's license. If you wish to make a whole-body donation, it is necessary to make prior arrangementswith a medical school.

After organ and tissue donation, you still need to make funeral arrangements. If arrangements have been made for your body to be donated to a medical school, the school will transport the body and assume responsibility for disposal by cremation. Depending on the school, the ashes may be returnedto your loved ones, who may not receive them for up to two years. Except for removing corneas, whole body donation usually precludes the donation of individual organs or tissues for transplants.

These are just a few of the deposition options available. Some less traditional options include natural burial (bodies are wrapped in a shroud or placed in a biodegradable casket, allowing the remains to decompose naturally), and promession, or "freeze-drying" (immersing the corpse in liquid nitrogen). Consult your local funeral director about local, state,and/or federal laws and regulations regarding funeral practices.

With so many options available, the decision about disposing of your body can be stressful for lovedones if they have no idea what your desires are.

Disposition of My Body (continued)

I would like:

- ☐ Embalming followed by burial

- ☐ Embalming followed by cremation

- ☐ Immediate burial

- ☐ Immediate cremation
- ☐ Other: _____

Special Instructions:

_____

_____

_____

_____

_____

_____

_____

_____

_____

_____

_____

_____

Disposition of Cremated Remains

Choosing cremation also requires decisions about the final disposition of cremated remains. Cremated remains are customarily returned to the loved ones in a cardboard or plastic container, unless an urn has been purchased and provided to the crematory or mortuary.

Urns are available in many styles, shapes, and sizes. Most mortuaries have a display and/or catalog of available choices.

Cremated remains can be buried in a cemetery lot, placed in an above-ground columbarium niche designed for cremated remains, buried at the base of a newly planted tree as part of a natural burial ground, or scattered or kept by loved ones. (Check state laws related to scattering cremated remains).

Most cemeteries allow one set of cremated remains and one casket to be buried in one lot, or two sets of cremated remains in one lot. Call or visit cemeteries to help make an informed decision.

Special Instructions:

_____

_____

_____

_____

_____

_____

_____

_____

_____

_____

Cemetery

There are four main types of cemeteries:

- *public cemeteries*: the most common type, which are for-profit cemeteries (i.e., independentlyor corporately owned);
- *religious cemeteries*: non-profit cemeteries owned by a religious organization;
- *district or municipal cemeteries*: non-profit cemeteries owned by a city/town or county;
- *national or veterans' cemeteries*: government-run cemeteries for the burial of veterans andtheir families.

If you choose to have a burial, choosing a cemetery and paying its fees in advance is something youcan do long before the need arises. Choosing your final resting place relieves your loved ones of having to make the otherwise difficult decision about whether you want to be:

a. buried where you are now;

b. buried near loved ones;

c. buried in another state; or,

d. buried in your hometown.

_____

Cemetery of choice

_____

Address

_____

City, State, Zip

_____

Phone

_____

Earth Burial   Mausoleum

_____

If pre-purchased, where can the paperwork be found?

Special Instructions:

_____

_____

_____

Grave Markers

Before purchasing a grave marker, find out the type of markers the cemetery of your choice will allow. Some allow only flat markers; others will allow upright or flat markers. Many mortuarieshave displays of available markers, or you can visit a monument company where they are made.

Markers can be made from many different materials: granite, marble, other types of stones, bronze,or other metals. A marker can be pre-purchased, inscribed with your name and birthdate, and installed at the cemetery, or your family can wait until the time of need to complete inscriptions.

Inscriptions can be as simple or as detailed as you desire. Pictures, emblems, or other details can beadded as well.

Marker selected and paid for: ☐ Yes   ☐ No

Marker already set: ☐ Yes   ☐ No

_____
If not already purchased, type of marker you prefer

_____
Special designs or inscriptions preferred

Other Instructions:

_____

_____

_____

_____

_____

_____

_____

_____

_____

_____

_____

Casket/Vault Selections

Today, caskets come in many shapes and colors, and are made from many materials, with a wide variety of interiors from which to choose. Your casket choice is no longer limited by what your chosenmortuary can provide; even retailers such as Walmart and Costco sell caskets online. In addition, there are artisans that can custom-design and build a casket for you.

Describe your casket preference:

_____

_____

_____

_____

_____

_____

Whether you choose in-ground burial, above-ground entombment, or cremation, every cemetery has its own requirements that need to be met before your wishes can be honored. It is best to consult with a cemetery director for advice.

Preparation of My Body

Burial Clothing

It is *your* funeral: You can wear anything *you* want. Taking the time now to document how youwant to be dressed is the best way to ensure that your wishes will be honored.

It can be stressful for your loved ones to have to go through your closet, deciding what youwould want to wear. Relieve that possible stress now, by making your choices known.

Describe the burial clothing you would prefer:

_____

_____

_____

_____

_____

Hair

Describe how your hair should be styled. A recent photo can be very helpful.

_____

_____

_____

Do you have a regular stylist who should be called to style your hair?   ☐ Yes   ☐ No

If yes, please give the name, phone number, and email address of the stylist:

_____
Name

_____
Phone number

_____
Email address

Cosmetics

Make-up instructions: foundation color, lipstick color, eye shadow, rouge, etc.:

_____

_____

_____

Fingernail polish? ☐ Yes ☐ No   Color:_____Brand: _____

Other cosmetics instructions:

_____

_____

_____

.

Jewelry

There are no state laws regarding whether jewelry may be buried with the deceased. Many peopleprefer to have jewelry on their body during visitation and funeral services, then removed before burial.

What is your jewelry preference?

_____

_____

_____

_____
Return jewelry to (name)

Part II:
Who Needs to Be Notified and What Needs to Be Stated?

Obituary Information

Newspapers and Notices

List the newspapers that you would like your obituary to appear. If the name of the newspaper is notknown, list the city and state. In addition to newspapers, think of publications such as business, community, or alumni journals; any place where there are people who should be aware of your death.

Newspaper Name	City, State
Newspaper Name	City, State
Newspaper Name	City, State
Newspaper Name	City, State
Newspaper Name	City, State

Obituary Photo

Some newspapers allow a photo of the deceased to be included with the obituary; some will chargean additional fee for this service.

Would you like a photograph included with your obituary?   ☐ Yes   ☐ No

If yes, attach your selected photograph to this booklet or indicate below where the photograph can be found:

_____

_____

_____

_____

Obituary Preparation

Your obituary is *your* life story; therefore, shouldn't *you* be the one who writes it? Writing your obituary ahead of time will save your loved ones the stress of trying to remember everything they believe was important to you. Either attach a copy of the obituary text you have written to this booklet or outline your thoughts below:

Obituary Text or Outline:

_____

_____

_____

_____

_____

_____

_____

_____

_____

_____

_____

_____

_____

_____

_____

_____

_____

_____

_____

_____

_____

_____

Obituary Details

Career Overview:

_____

_____

_____

Community Service:

_____

_____

_____

Membership in Service, Social, Professional, or Honorary Organizations:

_____

_____

_____

Military Service and Citations:

_____

_____

_____

Special Events, People, and Places:

_____

_____

_____

Church Information:

_____

_____

_____

Obituary Details (continued)

Special Accomplishments:

_____

_____

_____

Survivors

Spouse/Partner:

_____

_____

Parents:

_____

_____

Sons:

_____

_____

_____

Daughters:

_____

_____

_____

Stepchildren:

_____

_____

_____

Survivors (continued)

Brothers:

_____

_____

_____

Sisters:

_____

_____

_____

Stepbrothers and sisters:

_____

_____

_____

Grandchildren (by name or a number):

_____

_____

_____

Great-grandchildren (by name or a number):

_____

_____

_____

Others to be named:

_____

_____

_____

Obituary Details (continued)

Preceded in death by:

_____

_____

_____

_____

_____

_____

_____

Any other information not covered above:

_____

_____

_____

_____

_____

_____

_____

_____

_____

_____

Notifications

Loved ones may be unaware of the people or agencies to be notified of your death. Please list fullnames (middle initials, too), addresses, phone numbers, and email addresses of all who should benotified. If more space is needed, use the blank pages at the end of this document.

_____

Pastor

_____

Executor

_____

Attorney

_____

Accountant

_____

Financial Advisor

_____

Insurance Agent

_____

Insurance Agent

_____

Employer

_____

Retirement Plan

_____

Retirement Plan

_____

Retirement Plan

Notifications (continued)

_____
Veterans Administration

_____
Social Security

_____
Medicaid

_____
Bank

_____
Bank

_____
Bank

_____
Physician

Other notifications:

_____

_____

_____

_____

_____

_____

_____

_____

Family and Friends to Be Notified

List Full Name, Relationship, Address, Phone Number, and Email Address:

_____

_____

_____

_____

_____

_____

_____

_____

_____

_____

_____

_____

_____

_____

_____

_____

_____

_____

_____

_____

People Who Are NOT to Be Notified

List Full Name:

_____

_____

_____

_____

_____

_____

_____

_____

_____

_____

_____

_____

_____

_____

Part III:
Important Papers, Information, and Artifacts

(

Important Papers and Information

To thwart any attempt by others to assume control of your assets, it is strongly recommended that you keep all the following documents in one place **but separate from this document** (for example, in a file folder located in a bedroom or in a suitcase located in a closet):

- Your will or living trust
- Insurance information
- Bank information
- Information on who is the signatory on these accounts (i.e., name, address, phone number, email address)

- Loan Information
- Stocks, Bonds, Mutual Funds
- Mortgage/Deed(s):
- Credit Cards:
- Where do you keep bills to be paid
- Other Valuables

Special Instructions:

_____

_____

_____

_____

_____

_____

_____

_____

_____

_____

_____

_____

_____

Your Digital Information

Your electronic devices, email service, social media, online entertainment, online banking, and cloud-based documents and photographs all require digital access. There are password-management services, such as LastPass (www.LastPass.com) or Everplans (www.Everplans.com), that can maintain all your passwords. Another option is to list the contents of your digital estate below, tear this section out, and include it with your "Important Papers and Information" (see page 33).

Password Manager

Service: _____

Notes and Instructions: _____

_____

Electronic Devices

Phone   Access Code/Password: _____

Computer   Access Code/Password: _____

Laptop   Access Code/Password: _____

Tablet   Access Code/Password: _____

Other Devices

Device #1: _____ Access Code/Password: _____

Device #2: _____ Access Code/Password: _____

Cloud Storage Accounts (e.g., Dropbox, OneDrive, iCloud)

Service #1: _____ Login: _____ Password: _____

Service #2: _____ Login: _____ Password: _____

Service #3: _____ Login: _____ Password: _____

Digital Payment Services

PayPal   Username: _____   Password: _____

SquareUp   Username: _____   Password: _____

Venmo   Username: _____   Password: _____

Email Addresses

Address #1: _____   Login:_____   Password: _____

Address #2: _____   Login:_____   Password: _____

Address #3: _____   Login:_____   Password: _____

Address #4: _____   Login:_____   Password: _____

Entertainment Accounts (e.g., Netflix, Apple Music, PlayStation Plus)

Service #1: _____   Login: _____   Password: _____

Service #2: _____   Login: _____   Password: _____

Service #3: _____   Login: _____   Password: _____

Service #4: _____   Login: _____   Password: _____

Online Banking

Bank #1: _____   Login: _____   Password: _____

Bank #2: _____   Login: _____   Password: _____

Notes: _____

_____

_____

Social Media Accounts

Facebook   Username: _____   Password: _____

LinkedIn   Username: _____   Password: _____

Twitter   Username: _____   Password: _____

Other Social Media Accounts

Account: _____   Username: _____   Password: _____

Account: _____   Username: _____   Password: _____

Notes or Additional Information

_____

_____

_____

_____

_____

_____

_____

_____

_____

_____

_____

Memorabilia or Artifacts Disposal

You may have memorabilia or artifacts related to your membership in service, social, professional, or honorary organizations. It is a good idea to identify those items and leave specific instructions for their proper disposal or distribution.

Item #1:

Location: _____

How to properly dispose of item: _____

_____

Name of contact: _____

Address: _____

Phone number: _____ Email: _____

Item #2:

Location: _____

How to properly dispose of item: _____

_____

Name of contact: _____

Address: _____

Phone number: _____ Email: _____

Item #3:

Location: _____

How to properly dispose of item: _____

_____

Name of contact: _____

Address: _____

Phone number: _____ Email: _____

Item #4:

Location: _____

How to properly dispose of item: _____

_____

Name of contact: _____

Address: _____

Phone number: _____ Email: _____

Item #5:

Location: _____

How to properly dispose of item: _____

_____

Name of contact: _____

Address: _____

Phone number: _____ Email: _____

Item #6:

Location: _____

How to properly dispose of item: _____

_____

Name of contact: _____

Address: _____

Phone number: _____ Email: _____

Item #7:

Location: _____

How to properly dispose of item: _____

_____

Name of contact: _____

Address: _____

Phone number: _____ Email: _____

Part IV:
What Should Your Funeral Look Like?

Viewing the Body

Whether or not your body is viewed before or during the funeral service, and by whom, should be your decision; however, loved ones' level of comfort with that decision should be considered as well. While some choose not to have a viewing, others feel it can help loved ones move toward acceptance of your death. For some, a viewing provides time to reflect on memories and private thoughts.

I would like to have:

☐ a public viewing

☐ a private viewing (loved ones or invitation only)

☐ a fully open casket; or,

☐ a partially open casket (usually from the waist up)

☐ No viewing

Special Instructions:

_____

_____

_____

_____

_____

_____

_____

_____

_____

_____

_____

Funeral or Memorial Service

You can determine the type of service to have—or you may decide not to have a service. Thus, it is important that you document if you want a funeral or memorial service and, if so, what it should looklike.

Your options include:

☐ Full funeral service with viewing

☐ Full funeral service with no viewing

☐ Graveside service (no viewing)

☐ Memorial service after burial (no viewing)

☐ Viewing with no service

☐ No service or viewing

☐ Other—Special Instructions: _____

Location of service (address, contact person, phone number):

_____

_____

Services to be conducted by (name, address, phone number):

_____

_____

Eulogy or memorial statements by (name, address, phone number):

_____

_____

_____

_____

_____

_____

Pallbearers

Pallbearers carry or walk next to the casket from the hearse to the gravesite. In a military or dignitary'sfuneral, they may carry or walk with the casket during a processional. If the pallbearers will carry the casket, they must be physically able to do so.

Traditionally, there are six to eight pallbearers. Honorary pallbearers who are not physically able tocarry the casket may also be appointed.

Pallbearers (names, addresses, phone numbers):

_____

_____

_____

_____

_____

_____

_____

Honorary Pallbearers (names, addresses, phone numbers):

_____

_____

_____

_____

_____

_____

_____

_____

Readings

Select favorite passages of scripture, poems, or literary passages to be read at your funeral or memorial service:

_____

_____

_____

List names, addresses, and phone numbers of who will perform readings at your service:

_____

_____

_____

Music

What type of music and songs should be played at your service? Do you want an organist or vocalist?Maybe you want an acapella group or a cultural dance troupe to perform? Maybe you can record a playlist of your favorite songs to be played before, during, or after the service. Document what you would like below.

Favorite Songs:

_____

_____

_____

Musicians (names, addresses, phone numbers):

_____

_____

Vocalists (names, addresses, phone numbers):

_____

_____

Flowers and Donations

Do you want flowers at your funeral or memorial service? Perhaps you would prefer that mournerssend donations to a favorite charity in lieu of flowers; if so, be sure to document that information below.

Flower and Arrangements Preferences:

_____

_____

_____

_____

_____

_____

_____

Preferred Florist (name, address, phone number):

_____

_____

_____

Church and/or Charities to Receive Memorial Donations (name, address, phone number):

_____

_____

_____

_____

_____

_____

Service Program

A service program usually presents, in printed format, the obituary, the order of the service, the list ofspeakers, and the music for the service. The program should reflect your style and personality in a meaningful way. As service programs are often saved as keepsakes by loved ones and guests, this program will be a memorable way to remember your style and spirit. You can personalize your program with your favorite pictures, art, graphics, quotations, religious verses, poems, or special readings.

Program Preferences:

_____

_____

_____

_____

_____

_____

Memorial Table

A memorial table holds photos, crafts, stories, newspaper clippings, and other memorabilia from yourlife. The display helps to personalize the service and invites conversation and reminiscences. Loved ones and guests can be asked to bring mementoes to place on the memorial table or to share with other loved ones and guests. The table can be set up at a funeral or memorial service, post-service event, or at a loved one's home.

Memorial Table Preferences:

_____

_____

_____

_____

_____

_____

Video

You may want to make a video of yourself at home, work, or attending special events. The video could also be a montage of your favorite foods, images, trips, hobbies, activities, etc. If you decide to make avideo of yourself, use the space below to document what you want to capture in that video.

Video Preferences:

_____

_____

_____

_____

Post-Service Event

A post-service event can be held in a loved one's home, in a reception area, or perhaps your favoriterestaurant. Indicate below the type of post-service event you would prefer.

What type of event would you prefer?

_____

_____

Where will the event be held (name, contact, address, phone number)?:

_____

_____

Who are the event planners (names, contacts, addresses, phone numbers)?:

_____

_____

_____

_____

_____

Part V:
Special Notes to My Loved Ones

Special Notes to My Loved Ones

Use the space below to explain or say, in death, what you were not able to express in life:

_____

_____

_____

_____

_____

_____

_____

_____

_____

_____

_____

_____

_____

_____

_____

_____

_____

_____

_____

_____

_____

Special Notes to My Loved Ones (continued)

Use the space below to explain or say, in death, what you were not able to express in life:

_____

_____

_____

_____

_____

_____

_____

_____

_____

_____

_____

_____

_____

_____

_____

_____

_____

_____

_____

Part VI:
Options for Veterans

Options for Veterans

If you are a veteran, information from your veteran's service records and/or discharge papers may be required to apply for the following services. Such records can be obtained from the National Personnel Records Center. (Note: It can take up to 6 months to receive the records.) For more information, contact the Department of Veterans Affairs National Cemetery Administration at https://www.cem.va.gov.

Burial Benefits and Memorial Items: To find out how to apply for burial benefits earned and how to plan for a burial in advance or at the time of need, visit:
https://www.va.gov/burials-memorials

Honor a Veteran or Reservist with Memorial Items: While planning a burial for a veteran or reservist, a loved one can apply for certain memorial items to honor their military service. An eligible spouse or other family member buried in a national cemetery or certain other veteran or military cemeteries may also qualify for a headstone or marker to identify the place of burial. Visit https://www.va.gov/burials-memorials/memorial-items or call (800) 698-2411 (TTY:711).

Burial with Military Honors: The rendering of military funeral honors for an eligible veteran, free of charge, is mandated by law. To learn about eligibility for this service, visit https://www.military.com/benefits/burial-and-memorial/military-funeral-honors.html

Resources

Batesville. (n.d.). *Decisions you'll make.*
https://www.batesville.com/helping-families/decisions-youll-make

Brasler, K. (2017). *Options for body disposition after death.*
https://www.checkbook.org/national/funeral-homes/articles/Options-for-Body-
Disposition- After-Death-28

Everplans. (n.d.). *Places that will take care of your pet if something happens to you.*
https://www.everplans.com/articles/places-that-will-take-care-of-your-pet-if-
something-happens-to-you

Everplans. (2018). *Pre-planning: How to choose a cemetery.*
https://www.everplans.com/articles/pre-planning-how-to-choose-a-cemetery

Marsden-Ille, S. (2021, November 19). *Aquamation or resomation: A "green" alternative to
the traditional funeral.* U.S. Funerals Online. https://www.us-
funerals.com/aquamation-or-resomation/#.YdOwzGjMKUk

Pappas, S. (2011). *After death: 8 burial alternatives that are going mainstream.*
https://www.livescience.com/15980-death-8-burial-alternatives.html

Weisbord R. K., & Horton D. (2021, May 19). 68% of Americans do not have a will. *The
Conversation.* https://theconversation.com/68-of-americans-do-not-have-a-will-
137686

Access to the Fillable PDF

Thank you for your purchase. To receive a fillable PDF version of this funeral planning guide, please send an email to Lisa@DrLisaOliver.com. You can also scan the QR code below which will take you to my email address. Please include a photo of your receipt. Thank you.

Lisa Caraway Oliver, EdD, GC-C
Life Transitions Educator | Certified Grief Counselor

A life transitions educator and certified grief counselor, Dr. Lisa Caraway Oliver educates individuals about life transitions and their residual effects: grief, mourning, and bereavement. Through this education, individuals are empowered to make informed decisions concerning advanced-care plans and are guided toward comprehending feelings and actions that occur because of a loss. The passion for this work emanates from a desire to mitigate the generational dysfunction that can occur when families postpone discussions on these inevitable topics.

Dr. Oliver earned her Doctor of Education in Adult Education from the University of Georgia, where, within the framework of death and dying, emotion work, and informal learning, she researched the work of hospice care professionals. She earned her Master of Science in Instructional Technology from Georgia State University and her Bachelor of Science in Electrical Engineering from Howard University. Dr. Oliver earned her certification in grief counseling from the American Academy of Grief Counseling.

Dr. Oliver facilitates, with fellow parishioner Sharyn M. Hailey, the Life Transitions Education Series at St. Paul's Episcopal Church and is a facilitator of Walking the Mourner's Path, an 8-week, Christ-centered grief ministry. She also facilities Death Cafes and a Life Transitions Education Series throughout the community via the Fulton County and Gwinnett County Library Systems. Dr. Oliver has also coordinated, with other like-minded parents and grandparents, a "Free Hugs" campaign at the Black Atlanta Pride Community Festival and the Atlanta Pride Parade.

A native of Atlantic City, New Jersey, Dr. Oliver resides in Atlanta, Georgia with her husband Jeff, their two adult children, two messy dogs, one vocal cat, and a bearded dragon.

Find out more about Dr. Oliver and her work on her website: www.DrLisaOliver.com.

www.ingramcontent.com/pod-product-compliance
Lightning Source LLC
Chambersburg PA
CBHW080401030426

42334CB00024B/2958